Wild Amazing Africa

KITSAP
PUBLISHING

Amazing and While Africa – Journal of a Photo Safari
First edition, published 2021

By Cindy Rasmussen
Cover images provided by Cindy Rasmussen
Copyright © 2021, Cindy Rasmussen

Hardbound ISBN-978-1-952685-33-0

Published by Kitsap Publishing
P.O. Box 572
Poulsbo, WA 98370
www.KitsapPublishing.com

50-10 9 8 7 6 5 4 3 2 1

Wild Amazing Africa

Journal of a Photo Safari

Cindy Rasmussen

Preface

WHAT IS IT ABOUT AFRICA?

Africa, the second largest continent on the globe, encompassing 11.7 million square miles, is vast, diverse, and enigmatic. It evokes emotions of wonder and fascination and has been the inspiration of such classics as Earnest Hemingway's book, "The Snows of Kilimanjaro," and the 1985 classic film "Out of Africa." As have many before us, my husband, Phil, and I had long dreamed about taking an African safari sometime in the future. So, one sunny day in July, we found ourselves seriously discussing the prospect of taking such a trip. We proceeded to locate a travel agency that specialized in African safaris and began to plan this much-anticipated journey. We chose a company that focused on small group travel and expected 6-10 others to share the trip with us. As it turned out, we were the only ones who signed up for the particular dates for this trip, and we had to decide if we wanted to pay a higher price for a private safari or else wait for another opportunity when more people signed up to go. Our travel planner, Jodi, strongly advised us to take the trip privately, stating that it was such a fantastic experience that we would never regret paying a bit more to go by ourselves. We decided to take her advice, and as she correctly predicted, it exceeded all expectations and became the amazing journey of a lifetime that will remain in our memories forever!

THE PREPARATION

The departure date was set for January 15th. We had five months to prepare, and we were savoring every moment of the prep time. Half the fun of any adventure is the anticipation, and this trip was no exception. We had certain necessary tasks to complete, such as making sure that our passports were current; they were, and making sure that we had all of the required vaccines; we didn't. One of the more enjoyable tasks was assembling proper wardrobes, which required several trips to REI, a recreational outlet store in Seattle, and the purchase of far too many clothes by me. Phil was more conservative, purchasing only what he really needed. Finding the right camera equipment and learning to use it was also a challenging adventure. Mark, our professional photographer son, had advised us about which camera was "the best" in hopes that we would be tempted to purchase it and then trade cameras with him upon our return; we took the bait. The camera was a Nikon D-300 with a vibration reduction wide-angle/zoom lens. The only catch was that this camera was so new on the market that it literally was not available anywhere in the U.S. The local camera store had ONE CAMERA, which we could look at but it was not for sale. The two major photo supply retailers, both located on the east coast, did not have any of these cameras available either. I ordered from one of these, letting them know that if we couldn't get it before January 14th (it was now the end of December), then we wouldn't need it and would cancel the order. As if a magic wand was waved, the camera was delivered in about a week. Our other purchase was a Sony Camcorder, of lesser quality and expense, but perfect for our trip. We then, of course, needed all of the requisite gear like camera cases, lenses, tripods, and night lights, not to mention extra memory, larger batteries, charging equipment, and on and on. Then we had to learn how to use all of this equipment. Phil was assigned the camcorder, as he had become quite proficient with making movies of our adventures. I took on the still camera, which fortunately had some automatic settings that I hoped would do a fantastic job without too much expertise on my part. We also purchased several books on the identification of animals and tried to learn a little about their habits and habitat, all of which would be promptly forgotten in the excitement of the first actual wild animal sighting. So, loaded down with all of our new gear and lightened up in the wallet, we were ready for the big adventure. It was amazing to us how quickly these five months passed, and before we knew it, we were on the plane bound for Kilimanjaro.

THE JOURNEY

Phil and I have traveled extensively, and every trip we took I always vowed to keep a journal. I made faithful entries for the first few days or so, then "fizzled out" on the project, relying later on pictures and memories alone. This time I was determined to keep an accurate journal; memories have a way of fading and playing tricks on us, so what follows is the day by day account that I kept of our wonderful trip to this amazing land.

The
Day-by-Day
Journal

JANUARY 16

We left Seattle just after lunch and arrived in Amsterdam some ten hours later. From there we flew to our destination; Kilimanjaro Airport, Arusha, Tanzania, Africa arriving at about 9 P.M., a day later. The first order of business after arrival was obtaining a visa at the airport. We were tired and had been slow disembarking the airplane, so we were at the end of the visa line. The line had approximately 100+ people with a 5 minute per person processing time. Movement through the line was excruciatingly slow for the first hour. Suddenly two or three helpers arrived, and the line finally diminished until it got to us. After obtaining the visas, we walked outside the airport where we were met by our driver, Godson, who was concerned that maybe we had lost our luggage or some other disaster since it took us so long to get through the airport process. He explained to us that getting visas does not usually take so long. Godson, a very tall, fairly good-looking young man led us to his vehicle, which was a large Toyota safari van. By large, I mean that it had three rows of seats behind the driver and a large rear trunk area, with the capability of seating a good ten people plus the driver. My thought was they must have been short on vehicles for making the airport pick-up run and that we would see a much smaller safari jeep later. The drive to our hotel in Arusha took another hour, and Godson tried to entertain us along the way by pointing out local landmarks in the dark, which was totally lost on us after the exhausting 24-hour plane trips. We finally checked into our hotel, made some rather incoherent plans about talking to Godson the next day, and more or less collapsed into our beds and into a sound sleep.

JANUARY 17

We spent this day just relaxing at The New Arusha Hotel. After eating a buffet breakfast, we walked outside in the garden and had an impromptu "tour" given to us by a tall, slender African with many missing teeth, who wore a badge reading "head gardener." He was very friendly and proud of his knowledge of the local plants in the large hotel garden. He spoke reasonably good English, told us he was of Maasai ancestry, but he really liked to play golf and tennis and most definitely was not into the "cultural thing."

Phil had earlier broken a fingernail and needed some nail clippers, which of course we did not have due to airline regulations, so we needed to find a pair locally. The quest for this item turned out to be a significant challenge. There were none in the small hotel shop, which meant venturing outside of the hotel grounds. We had noted earlier that the hotel was surrounded by concertina wire, and the entrance was guarded by armed security personnel. It took us all of two minutes to understand the reason for the security once we left the grounds. We were immediately accosted by what were known locally as "flycatchers," who wanted to escort us across the street, or to the local shops, or sell us local goods, or anything that might produce some American dollars for them. Once we got several blocks away from the hotel perimeter, the flocks of "flycatchers" disappeared, but it took us many blocks of walking into numerous shops before we finally found a pair of nail clippers. They were made in Korea and didn't cut nails at all, but Phil struggled until he succeeded in clipping at least the errant nail.

After completing this task, we decided to spend the rest of the day on hotel grounds. I managed to do some shopping in the hotel where I found a source of Tanzanite. Arusha is the Tanzanite capital of Africa, as it is only found in this location, and the large mine is a major local employer. The hotel was an official outlet for sales of the stone to tourists, and Tanzanite was on my list of purchases. The sales lady was European and very knowledgeable about the stones, so we purchased a pair of matched stones for earrings. We were stunned about the price of these stones and also the large variation in quality. It is similar to purchasing a diamond, and in fact, we did receive a certificate of authenticity with an exact description of the stones. We also purchased some T-shirts and some attractive wood carvings. The rest of the day we spent watching TV, napping, reading, and practicing the use of our cameras in the garden.

JANUARY 18

Godson arrived to pick us up at the hotel at about 9 A.M. After clearing up some minor issues, we were ready to begin the first day of our long-anticipated safari. When Godson led us to the waiting safari vehicle, we were amazed to learn that the same very large vehicle that had picked us up at the airport would be our private safari vehicle for the entire trip! Godson occupied the front seat with his equipment and the lunches, and Phil and I had three rows of seats from which to select the best view and/or most comfortable seat. We learned during the safari that there were two opening hatches, and we could stand on different seats for better viewing and photos, so we ended up really appreciating all of this extra room.

Our first visit on the safari was to Arusha National Park, which was the closest in distance to the town of Arusha, where we had stayed upon our arrival. Arusha National Park was very nice and very quiet. We only saw three or four other vehicles while driving all day in the park. We drove some distance before seeing any animals, and we had a discussion with Godson about whether or not we would see any animals at all that day. He laughed and assured us that we would absolutely see lots of giraffes. Our first sighting of animals was a distant herd of giraffes, zebras, and cape buffalo. After that, we drove for quite some time in the forest looking for colobus monkeys, but all we saw were butterflies. Later we saw some dik-diks, a very small antelope-type animal. Finally, we left the forest and came into a large grassy opening with several watering holes where we saw warthogs, many with babies, also giraffes, and zebras. In addition, there were waterbucks and more cape buffalo, many with babies and all very close, so we were able to get many good pictures.

Cape Buffalo and Warthog

Upper: Colobus Monkeys / Lower: Vervet Monkeys

Soon, we came to a lake where we stopped for lunch, sitting on rocks by the side of the lake. We had box lunches with way too much food, and our guide, Godson, was happy to take any leftovers we couldn't eat to give to his friends. We were soon to discover that nothing goes to waste in Africa, and we were happy to share our food with Godson, which he passed along to those who were in need. As we drove out of the park, we finally came across the difficult-to-find but beautiful colobus monkeys. They are a striking black and white color, with long flowing tails, and almost appear to fly as they traverse from tree to tree in the forest. Finally, we saw a very large number of baboons in a tree on the side of the road. This group included families, and many mothers with babies who were riding underneath their mothers' tummies.

After leaving Arusha National Park, Godson took us to visit a school just outside of Arusha, as per a request from us the previous day. Although we were reluctant to ask for deviations from the prepared itinerary, a long-time friend, Marion Sluys, told us about his special missionary school in Tanzania, which he and his wife visited annually. He had given us specific directions about finding it, so we promised him we would make a visit when we were there. It proved more challenging to find the school than any of us had anticipated, but Godsen was persistent, asking numerous pedestrians along the roadside until we finally found it. It was in a beautiful setting, high up on a hill overlooking the valley below. The school itself was much larger than Phil and I had imagined it to be. We also thought it included an orphanage, but found this not to be true. School was out for the day, but we did see a few of the remaining students heading home. We met the director and headteacher who gave us a short tour of some of the classrooms as well as one of their administrative buildings. The classrooms were very sparse, but education in Africa is highly valued, and the teachers were very proud of their facilities. Phil and I gave them a donation, which we knew would be put to good use.

After leaving the school, we drove to our first overnight destination of the safari, a private reserve on Mt. Kilimanjaro's west side, the Nkwardako Ranch. We were soon to discover that Tanzania has a total of five national parks, several national reserves, and also private reserves. The rules are different for all of these; there are absolutely no guns or weapons allowed in the national parks, and no one except the park rangers is allowed to exit a vehicle. Vehicles are required to stay on the gravel roads at all times, and the parks are cleared except for designated campsites, with no driving allowed after sunset. In the national reserves the animals are still protected but these are occupied by various local tribes who have been there forever. Many Maasai Villages are also located in the national reserves.

Finally, there are camps, ranches, and reserves that are held as private property owned primarily by foreigners and made available to tourists on safaris. Weapons are allowed on private property, and big game hunting is still permitted in some places. However, the places we visited were for photo safaris only. These places offered the unique opportunity to go on foot and also to take night drives, where nocturnal animals could be viewed in their habitats.

The Nkwardako Ranch was privately owned. It was exceptionally beautiful and was perhaps my favorite place on the entire trip. It had permanent tents that were the the circular African style Bomos, scattered throughout the wooded area. We had a private tent, which was as large as a small house, and included bathroom facilities. There was no electricity, only a solar generator which was turned off at night, so we had kerosene lanterns and flashlights after dark. Hot water was supplied by being heated on a fire, then being carried in buckets to our shower, which was a large bucket operated by pulling a cord to pour the water out to take a shower. Everywhere we stayed, the beds were surrounded by mosquito netting, but we never saw any mosquitos, just lots of flies in some places. As each tent was located in a private forested setting, we had several different types of game such as bushbucks that grazed in the clearing outside of our tent. The ranch had a large open-air dining room and lounge area, which was beautifully decorated in an African motif.

The only other guests at the time we were there were a German couple. We visited with them over cocktails before dinner and invited them to share dinner with us. However, we soon learned that since we had paid for a private safari, that was what we were going to receive, including all of our meals. The staff made it quite clear that the custom was for us to share dinner with our guide, and the Germans would be eating with theirs. We, of course, enjoyed our meals with Godson, and it gave us the opportunity to get to know him better.

After dinner, we had our first night drive, which turned out to be quite exciting and fun. The night drive was in an open jeep and included a driver and a "spotter." We had a talented spotter, and our little crew was quite determined that we would see animals on this drive, so see we did! We found an African cat, a mongoose, some zebras still grazing at night, and finally, a beautiful genet in a tree, a member of the cat family. After the drive—bedtime. It was a long day and we slept very well.

JANUARY 19

In the morning we had an early wake-up call, with coffee served on the porch outside of our tent, followed by hot showers with the bucket. This is a unique experience and felt really good after our long travels of the day before. While waiting for breakfast in the dining tent, we saw a large African cat run across the open space in front of the tent. After breakfast we went on a "bush walk" with Thomas, our armed walking guide.

Examining Prints and Scat

As we were soon to learn, you do not walk outside in Africa unless you are accompanied by someone who is armed. This was especially true at night but also held true during the daytime away from populated areas, such as on the private game reserves. Although Thomas was armed, he told us that he has never had to fire his gun in 13 years of walking. We hope he knew how, but his record held true for our walk, too. We saw several herds of zebras, some wildebeests, and several herds of impalas. We also watched mongoose hunting and hiding in their burrows. All of the animals we saw ran away as soon as they spotted us, but we did get a few good photos.

We stopped at an observation deck on our way back and met a young man from Georgia who was doing graduate work in animal biology. His goal was teaching it and he was spending a year in Africa. He had grown up in Chad and had wanted to come back to Africa. It is a place that seems to have a magic pull for those who have ever visited or lived here.

After lunch in the dining tent, we went with Thomas to visit an authentic Maasai village. I call it "an authentic Maasai village" because we were to learn later that there are tourist Maasai villages that are quite a different experience than this one. Our visit to this village was by itself worth the trip to Africa. Thomas explained that these villages are called BOMA's, an acronym for "British Overseas Military Administration." Each village consists of one-room mud huts arranged in a circular pattern, surrounded by a fence of Acacia Tree branches. The branches have long, sharp thorns which keep out predators, especially lions. Each village is occupied by a single family consisting of related males, each of whom has a number of wives and their children. Each wife builds her own mud hut, which consists of sticks on the inside layer mudded together with cow dung. In the center of the huts is a corral for livestock which is also protected by an Acacia Tree fence. The livestock consists of cattle, sheep, and goats. The sheep and goats are eaten and milked, but the cattle are only milked except when slaughtered for special ceremonies. The livestock is herded to grass and watering areas during the day and brought back to the BOMA at night for protection. Additionally, there are dogs at the BOMA, also for the protection of people and livestock. The women and children do all of the work, and wealth is measured by the number of cattle one owns. Wives are procured by the trading of cattle, so a rich man has many wives and many cattle.

Some additional notes about this village: It was thick with flies that landed on people's faces and in their hair. Phil and I could hardly stand it, but we were told that it didn't bother the villagers because they were used to it. Walking inside the compound, particularly the animal corral, was particularly unpleasant due to the animal waste mixed with the mud that stuck to our shoes. There was a large fence at the back of the corral which was adorned with numerous earrings, necklaces, and bracelets. When we asked Thomas about this fence, he explained that the women all shared their jewelry and that they could choose items from the community fence. All of the Maasai wear beautiful, colorful clothing and robes, and the women wear the ornate jewelry and earrings. Men also have pierced ears, and all tribespeople have the distinct elongated earlobes from wearing the earrings. Although our guide, Godson, had not wanted us to visit this village, Thomas had been quite insistent about taking us, and we are so glad to have had that opportunity. We stayed there for a long time and were able to watch the animals being herded home for the night. We noted that really young children were involved in that activity. Before we left, we also observed some of the men returning in their newer-looking trucks and jeeps from places unknown. Thomas didn't tell us where they had been all day, and we didn't ask.

JANUARY 20

After breakfast we said goodbye to the staff at Nkwardaki Ranch and proceeded to Tarangire National Park, arriving at about noon. This park is larger than Arusha, and it took two days to see all of it. On this day we saw our first herd of elephants, including a tiny week old baby at the watering hole with his mother. During the day, we also saw waterbucks, more zebras and giraffes, and lots of members of the antelope family, including dik-diks and impalas. We also saw our first ostriches and were surprised at how large they are. The birds in Africa are beautiful and we saw many different varieties over the days of animal viewing in these parks.

Impalas

Dik Dik

The vegetation is also impressive and unique. We saw the famous Baobab Trees, which we recognized from replicas at Disneyworld. In addition we saw Candelabra Trees, Sausage Trees, and Acacias. I think the most impressive thing about Africa is the vast landscape filled with literally thousands of animals co-existing in this wild land. It is difficult for us to imagine any place on earth that is so vast, so wild, so unpopulated, and seemingly untouched by man. Yet, here it was it in front of our eyes, and more than we ever imagined it would be.

Termite Mound

Baobob Tree

Candelabra Tree

Sausage Tree

Acacia Tree

While we were watching the elephants at the watering hole, we got inundated with an African rainstorm. It poured down heavily for about twenty minutes, then the sun came out again, and you would never believe it had rained. Godsen was particularly looking for some of the big cats on this day, but we did not see any. We left the park in the late afternoon and arrived at our next overnight destination, Kikoti Camp, another private camp, which we thoroughly enjoyed. It was located on a ridge looking across the Rift Valley at the Western Escarpment. Once again, we had our own private tent; this one was elevated and had indoor plumbing as well as solar-powered electricity. After our dinner in the beautiful open-air dining tent, we were escorted to our tent by an armed camp staff person. We were told that this requirement was due to possible encounters with elephants, cape buffalo, lions or hyenas, none of which we saw or heard during our stay in this camp.

JANUARY 21

Today, after breakfast, we returned to Tarangire Park for another day. Godson's goal on this day was to find a leopard. We were soon to learn that the leopard is probably the most elusive of the African animals. He is extremely well camouflaged, is primarily a nocturnal hunter, and sleeps during the day high up in the trees where he appears to be part of the branching system. Sometimes, all that can be spotted is a tail or legs hanging out of the tree. In the quest for a leopard, Godson chose a particular driving path that was well off the beaten track. We were driving over what he described as a "black cotton soil" road that was impassible and became a swamp in the rainy season. We did find several cheetahs early in the day, our first sighting of any big cats. The "off-road" driving up and down steep gullies was exciting, but no leopards were spotted. We also saw other game, most of which we had seen on earlier drives; but there was one exception, the spotting of a Kudu, which Godson said was especially fun for him to see, as sightings were rare.

We returned to Kikoti Camp late in the afternoon, but in time for a walk with 3 armed guides to a place called "Viewpoint." Two of our guides were armed with elephant rifles; the third was introduced as a "bushman" and was armed with a large bow and arrows, bushman style. The walk took Phil and me about an hour instead of the usual 1.5 hours it apparently took for most others. Along the way we observed tracks and "scat" from various animals, notably hyenas and elephants, but we did not see any of these animals. The "Viewpoint" was a covered platform located above a wide valley, where we could observe elephants and cape buffalo in the distance. Eventually, we heard an elephant approach more closely, but he did not ever get close enough for us to see him.

We had fun visiting with our guides, only one of whom could speak English, but we found out that all of them had a good understanding of it when we told the joke about the elephant who came for dinner and sat anywhere he wanted to. They all understood the joke and laughed heartily. This little excursion included cocktails at sunset at the Viewpoint, and we wondered how this would be accomplished, as no one had carried any drinks with us on the walk. Well, not too long after our arrival at the Viewpoint, a jeep drove up and delivered our "sundowners" with peanuts, which we enjoyed while watching the sunset. We were then driven back to camp. We marveled about our "Safari in style"!

The following day we asked Godson about the need for armed escorts everywhere, as we had yet to see any threatening animals on our various walks. Godson informed us that "Oh yes, the armed escorts were absolutely essential, and that there had been lions at the Viewpoint to greet the guests who had gone the day before us." Whew!!! There would be more surprises in store for us in this astonishing land. Our day was completed with an after-dinner night drive of about 45 minutes, during which we observed a nocturnal hare and a herd of impalas but no predators.

JANUARY 22

We left Kikoti Camp in the morning and headed for Lake Manyara National Park. This park is relatively small compared to all of the others and is primarily a "birder's paradise." We only spent a few hours here and mainly saw baboons and birds, the exception being one lone hippo in the river spotted by Phil. An elephant considered the possibility of joining us for lunch, then thought the better of it and walked away.

Birds of Africa

Yellow Billed Storks

Helmeted Guinea Fowl

Grey Crowned Crane

Black Headed Weaver

Secretary Bird

Superb Starling

Split Tail Kite

Yellow Billed Kite

Pelicans

Saddle Billed Stork

African Ibis

Yellow Billed Stork

African Eagle

After leaving Lake Manyara, we proceeded towards Ngorongoro Crater. When we stopped to check-in at the park gate, there were dozens of baboons, and Godson warned us to make sure that the doors and windows to the safari vehicle were closed, as otherwise the baboons would climb in and were very difficult to remove. Apparently they received food from tourists at this entrance and had become too tame and bold. We then drove to the top of the crater and along the rim, which provided spectacular views across and into the crater. We passed the luxury hotel where Bill Gates had stayed on a visit to Africa and arrived at our Serena Hotel close to dinner time. Serena Hotel was truly beautiful and luxurious to us. We had a room with a private balcony overlooking the crater.

JANUARY 23

Today was very special; we drove to the bottom of the Ngorongoro Crater and spent an entire day in this vast basin filled with nearly every species of animal that lives in Africa. These animals never leave the crater, and for this reason they are readily visible and easy to observe. It is accessed via a narrow and steep one-way road into the crater and another narrow, steep one-way road out again. Due to the fact that there are so many animals here, and they are so easily observed, there are also large numbers of safari vehicles and tourists taking advantage of the photo ops. For this reason, the park officials are starting to limit the number of daily visits to the crater, so we felt fortunate to have had the privilege of visiting. All of our other days in these parks were much more deserted in terms of tourists and vehicles, but this visit was well worth the time and effort, as some of these animals are rarely seen outside of Ngorongoro. It was here that we saw our first lions, several large males with a "kill." Two of the lions had eaten their fill and decided to leave the scene, walking right behind our vehicle as they crossed the road. All of the animals in the crater are accustomed to seeing the safari vehicles and are not frightened by them, nor do they pay any attention to them. However, we are told that it would be very dangerous to exit a vehicle, as many animals would not hesitate to attack a human on foot. The third lion decided to protect his kill from the hyenas and jackals that were surrounding him. He tried to drag it off, but after a while he gave it up and moved on. Godson told us that a single lion, even one as large as this particular male, is no match for a pack of hyenas.

We then moved on to a large watering hole where there were numerous animals, including hippos, zebras, wildebeests, jackals, and others. It was amazing to see this wide variety of animals peaceably occupying the same space around the watering hole. It was made even more astounding by the vastness of the surrounding landscape.

Impala

Thompson's Gazelle

Common Reedbuck

Wildebeest

The rest of the afternoon we spent tracking down the rare and endangered black rhino. Godson said these are extremely rare outside of the park and there are only about 20 of them inside the crater. All of the guides are in communication with each other over mobile radios, and they cooperate and share information regarding rare sightings, so Godson had learned the location of one of these rhinos and was intent on making sure that we saw it. When we first spotted the rhino, he was very distant, but Godson encouraged us to be patient, telling us that if we waited long enough, he was sure the rhino would come much closer for us to observe. Unfortunately, the rhino was in the middle of a large dust bowl area, and the vehicles were required to stay on the road, so we were unable to approach him. It took several hours of waiting and also driving in a circle around the dust bowl each time the rhino changed position. Finally, a small dust storm started blowing, which chased the rhino closer to the edge of the road, where we had the opportunity to take absolutely sensational photos of this rare, endangered animal. I can't end this story without saying truthfully that Godson, Phil, and I all felt sorry for the rhino because he was quite bewildered at being surrounded by safari vehicles and not knowing which way to turn to get away. He is obviously a timid animal and was the only animal we saw that day that seemed to be afraid of the vehicles.

Black Rhino

On the drive out of the crater we came across a lion pride with about 5 cubs; they were so cute and so much fun to observe up close.

Before dinner we were entertained at the hotel by the local Maasai children doing a traditional circumcision ceremonial dance. The males take turns jumping as high as they can while the rest chant. Maasai are quite tall anyway, and these youngsters could jump to amazing heights. It was interesting to watch.

JANUARY 24

This morning we left for Olduvai Gorge (pronounced Oldupai), stopping at another Maasai village on the way. This village was for the tourists and was quite different from our first village visit. There were no flies, but we were immediately surrounded and overwhelmed by villagers thrusting their various wares in our faces. We were allowed to take a few photos, and we ultimately purchased several of the beaded bracelets. Godson was not pleased about this visit and had issues with the rate he had been charged for bringing us there, which apparently had been raised without the knowledge or permission of the tour company.

Phil particularly enjoyed the visit to Olduvai, which is the site of the Leakey's excavations and discoveries of early man. There are ongoing excavations, and while no one was present at the time of our visit, we did get to see the camp where the researchers stay when they are at the site conducting a "dig." There is also a fascinating museum, and we had a private lecture about the history of the site and the work of the Leakeys.

OLDUPAI GORGE
SITE MUSEUM
= KARIBU =
Altitude: ca 1400 mls.asl.

LOUIS AND MARY LEAKEY
60 Years of Field Work at Prehistoric Sites in Tanzania
Miaka 60 ya Utafiti Porini kwenye Sehemu za urithi wa historia Tanzania

Louis Leakey 1903–1972

Mary Leakey 1913–1996

TENDAGURU 1924

OLDUVAI GORGE / KORONGO LA OLDUVAI 1931–1984

     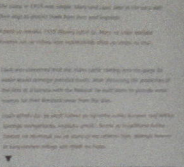 

The First Car to Reach Olduvai
Gari la kwanza kufika Olduvai

The Pioneers
Waanzilishi

The Road to Olduvai
Barabara ya kwenda Olduvai

Louis and Mary in the field at Olduvai / Louis na Mary wakiwa kwenye utafiti Olduvai

Discoveries / Ugunduzi: *Zinjanthropus* 1959

Discoveries / Ugunduzi: *Homo habilis* 1960

KONDOA 1951

LAETOLI 1976–1980

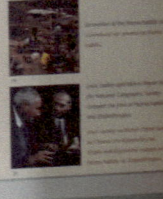

    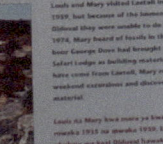   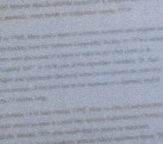 

  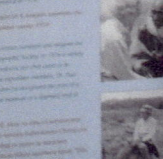 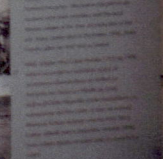

Leakey Excarvation Site

After leaving the gorge, Godsen had obtained permission to take us to another special place that was not on our itinerary but was a most interesting side trip. He took us to a location called "shifting sands," a large black horseshoe-shaped sand dune that indeed shifts intact over the years. There are permanent markers where measurements have been taken, showing movement of about 200 yards every five years of this entire intact dune.

Shifting Sands

After leaving "shifting sands" we proceeded to Serengeti National Park where we first saw the large migrating herds of wildebeest. We remembered a young photographer we had met when we first arrived, who was coming to film this migration, and at the time we didn't know that we would be able to see this as well, but on this day we saw both the migration of the vast herds, as well as a number of newborns at their mothers' sides.

This also turned out to be our day for the Big Cats. We first sighted some buzzards gathered around the remains of a "kill," which we could see was the leg of a baby zebra. A short distance away we could see two cheetahs, one lying in the shade of a bush with his head up and flicking at the flies. The other one was prone, lying very still about 10 yards away, nearly hidden in the grass. We were the only vehicle nearby, and so we were able to approach very close to the first cheetah under the bush. We took some beautiful pictures of him, then decided to see what the other one was doing. As we approached more closely, we were stunned to see that this one was dead. It was so sad; he was beautiful, just lying there without a mark on his body. There was absolutely no evidence of blood or injury, so we deduced that the mother zebra had tried to defend her young one and had apparently landed a successful strike to the head of this cheetah. Godson told us that these two cheetahs were probably young brothers, as normally these animals are solitary hunters, but young related males do sometimes hunt together. We left to drive around our circular route, and when we returned a Cheetah Research vehicle was on the site. The live cheetah had moved closer to the dead one but still seemed to be waiting for him to "wake up."

Baby Giraffe—Cheetah Kill

After driving a little further, we came upon a lion pride resting on the rocks in the afternoon sun; again there were mothers and cubs, and we were able to get good pictures.

The last sighting of the day was the prize we had been waiting for, the elusive leopard. A leopard had made a "kill" that he had placed at the base of a tree and he was attempting to drag it up the tree. We were about the 10th or 11th vehicle to arrive at the scene, so the leopard was well aware of the presence of all of these vehicles watching him. He decided to leave his "kill" at the bottom of the tree and climbed the tree. He moved around in the tree for a while, trying to get comfortable. He finally plopped himself into a sitting position in the crook of the tree with his back legs hanging down, and his front legs hooked like arms around the largest branch, just like a people!! It was so funny; everyone in all of the vehicles was laughing.

We waited about an hour for him to go down again and retrieve his "kill," but he was there for the duration, just waiting for all of us to go away. Maybe he knew the park rules, that we would all have to leave before sundown. At any rate, he had more patience than we did and was still in the tree when we left.

We arrived in time for dinner at the beautiful Serengeti Serena Lodge.

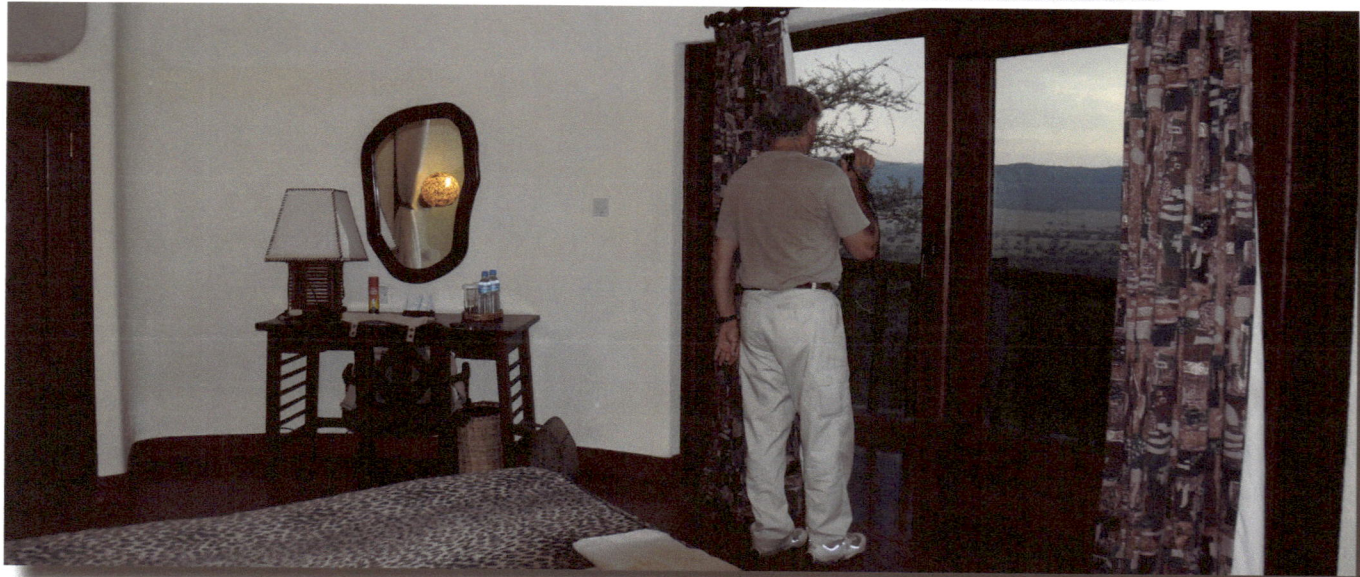

JANUARY 25

On this morning we went for a short game drive to a very large and active hippo pool where crocodiles coexisted with the hippos. On this particular morning the hippos were actively swimming about, getting in and out of the water with their babies, mouthing each other in mock fighting, and making lots of loud noises. We were able to take some excellent photos of all this activity, which Godsen told us was very rare. We returned to the lodge for lunch and then had some free time relaxing at the swimming pool before heading out again at 3 P.M.

This time we were going to our private tented camp on the Serengeti. This was another totally new and surprising experience for us. We had no idea what to expect when we passed a very large truck that had stopped beside the road with the hood raised and several men were peering inside at the engine.

Godson stopped and jumped out to check on it, returning to explain to us that this was our truck with the supplies for our mobile camp. Pretty soon, they closed the hood, decided it was OK, and proceeded on their way. Godson said they were going ahead of us to get set up and that we would be doing a game drive on our way to the camp. After seeing such prolific wildlife the day before, we were amazed at the vast expanse of land area that was now seemingly devoid of animals. The wildebeests had moved on but as we approached our campsite we did see some giraffes and impalas. We arrived at our campsite in time for cocktails and dinner, and we were absolutely amazed; this camp was beyond description, but I will try. When we had observed the large truck earlier, we were sure that we would be sharing this camp with others who were on safari with our same tour company. NOT!!! It was a camp only for us!!! Our private tent was by itself, located a short distance away from the communal tents. It literally had all of the comforts of home, including a carved toilet, washbasin, a separate shower compartment behind the bathroom compartment, and a front porch with a large hanging kerosene lamp and camp chairs. Near the center of the camp complex was the dining tent, complete with a bar. In front of that was a campfire with three chairs for Godson, Phil, and me to enjoy our after-dinner drinks and watch the stars. Off to the side and back was the outdoor kitchen area and the tent for the camp staff of six. We were truly "blown away" by this setup.

Godson got a kick out of helping in the kitchen, but otherwise, he got to kick back and enjoy the ambiance with us. We enjoyed a long visit with him under the stars that evening. After these many days of bouncing around all day in the safari jeep with him, we had become good friends and had shared a lot with each other about our lives. Godson was very proud of the fact that he was a Christian and also that he was educated and had a good job. He told us a little bit about his work history, how he had moved around to different companies for awhile, but was very happy in his current employment and had been there for a number of years. He told us he is 36 years old and single, but has a girlfriend and would like to get married sometime. He met his girlfriend at church; her parents were well known in the community, she is also educated and is an elementary school teacher. He speaks five languages, Swahili, English, French, Italian, and German. He lives with his mother and sister, who is still single. His father passed away within the last year, and he inherited some family money which he used to build several nice houses that he rented to foreigners. We knew that he took his job very seriously, he spoke good English, and put our needs, his customers, first at all times. He acted very professionally and took pride in the condition of his vehicle, taking excellent care of it even though it belonged to the company and was assigned to him. He also was very knowledgeable about the animals, their habitats, the flora and fauna of Africa, and the history of his country and its people. He told us he was trying to obtain a visa to visit the US. He had been turned down once before because they told him they were afraid he would not return to his own country as he didn't have enough "roots." That was before he owned property, so he was quite confident he would be able to get the visa this time around. Phil and I invited him to visit us if he did come to the US, and he told us he also had a friend in NY who had made the same offer. So after a long visit, we all turned in for the night. We heard a few strange noises that night, but for the most part slept very comfortably.

JANUARY 26

When Phil and I first planned this trip, Phil noted that Hot Air Balloon rides over the Serengeti were offered as a side trip. Our travel agent, Jodi, had confided to me earlier that she was not an enthusiastic supporter of the concept, and I was skeptical as well, but Phil really wanted to go, so we signed on for this excursion. The day had arrived, and we were awakened before dawn, at 5 AM, for the drive to the balloon launch site. There had been heavy rain the night before, so the crew was a little late getting started. We watched as they filled the two balloons with hot air, then we were instructed about how to climb into the baskets which were on their sides. We were stacked like mummies into the baskets, sixteen people in our balloon and twelve in the other one. Then the balloon slowly lifted and the baskets were turned right side up. We drifted over the Serengeti for about an hour, observing herds of animals from the air in the quiet balloons---an amazing experience! At one point the balloon came so close to the ground that it scraped the top of an Acacia tree, but was none the worse for the wear. We had light winds, and due to the good skills of our pilot, Nigel, we were able to land with the basket right side up, something that does not always occur, we were told. We were then served a champagne breakfast in the middle of the Serengeti, on tables replete with tablecloths and the "queen's silver"; another unforgettable experience!!

Upper Picture:Hyrax / Lower Picture: Leopard Tortoise

Left: Agame Lizard   /   Right: Hyrax

Godson picked us up after the balloon ride and took us for another short game drive. We returned to our camp for lunch and some rest before going on another late afternoon drive. Godson took us to view some unusual rock outcroppings, where large rocks were balanced on top of smaller ones.

He also took us to see a cave where there were primitive Maasai drawings and another site where there were "drum beating" rocks used by the Maasai, which left round chips in the rocks.

We returned to camp in time for dinner; we were tired and retired early. All was well until about 3 AM when I started to hear strange noises that sounded like large animals outside of our tent. I was debating whether or not to wake Phil when all of a sudden the side of the tent started to move. All I could think of was lions coming into the tent, so I started screaming at the top of my lungs. This did the trick; those animals were "outta there" dragging the heavy lantern on the front porch into the bush with them! Needless to say, the entire camp was awakened, and Godson came down in the safari vehicle to see if we were OK. He determined that it was hyenas, not lions, and they had most definitely been immediately outside of our tent. He made sure the tent was securely zipped closed, told us they couldn't get in, and everyone went back to bed. The hyenas were wailing and complaining loudly for a long time before finally fading into the distance. I didn't get any more sleep that night and was relieved that this was our last night in the tent. Godson told us the following day that he had not had an experience like that in his 13 years of being a guide, and it was extremely unusual for animals to approach the tent so closely and bump into it. Phil and I have determined that hyenas are every bit as nasty as lions, but we think they were really after some Impalas that were also in and around the camp that night. At any rate, this is one night that we will NEVER FORGET!!

JANUARY 27

We broke camp early this morning and started our drive to Lake Victoria. On the way we drove through the Western Serengeti, stopping at a favorite watering hole for crocodiles, but the water was high due to heavy rain the night before, so we only saw two very small crocs. We arrived at Lake Victoria at lunchtime, and at check-in, discovered that we would be unable to take the Dhow Boat ride, which was on our itinerary, due to afternoon storms on the lake. So we ate our packed lunch with Godson on the deck of our room which overlooked the beach and the lakefront. Then, Godson left to do his errands, and Phil and I were on our own until 4:30 when we were scheduled for a nature walk. The nature walk turned out to be "bird watching" with the husband of the hotel manager. The birds here are prolific, with many native species as well as migratory birds. It was interesting and fun until I felt painful stinging sensations up and down one of my legs. We had paused to observe a tree full of hanging nests, at which time the stinging ants had taken the opportunity to attack my left foot and leg. These ants stick to clothing and skin and are difficult to remove, so I made a hasty retreat to our quarters to change clothes and get rid of the ants. Thus ended the nature walk, "bird watching" experience. Earlier, we had seen the enormous tracks of some resident hippos on the beach at the lake. At just about dinner time, these hippos appeared and came out of the water to graze; three or four adults and a baby. Only in Africa would we be viewing grazing hippos from our dinner table!

JANUARY 28

Godson arrived right on time, bright and early in the morning, to take us for our final drive with him to meet the airplane that would fly us to Zanzibar. It was about a one-hour drive, but we had to re-enter the Serengeti Park with a paperwork delay. While we waited for Godson to complete the required paperwork, some monkeys surrounded our vehicle, trying to get into it, looking for food. Phil and I were taking turns visiting the restroom, one of us guarding while the other was gone. These monkeys are adept at squeezing through very small openings, and while Phil was distracted taking pictures of them, one managed to squeeze in through a window. The others then distracted Phil further by feigning an attack. They ran at him making "boxing" motions; it was hilarious. Finally, I arrived and tried to persuade the monkey in the car to get out. He was now perched on the open window, then finally jumped out and feigned an attack on me while I was climbing in the car to close the windows. These monkeys are quite small, but we were afraid they might bite. We must have looked really silly because some park staffers sitting at a nearby table all laughed and said, "they are teasing you." When Godson returned his first concern was whether or not they had taken our food, the three lunches on the front seat. Godson likes to eat!! When I asked if the monkeys would bite us, he replied, "only if they are cornered." As we were leaving we passed yesterday's hippo and croc river and today we had a good sighting of two or three crocs sunning themselves. After this we had to hurry to catch our 10 A.M. plane flight.

Vervet Monkeys

Final Day with Godson

Even our exit from Serengeti was a surprise. We had been expecting an hour or so delay at some small airport where we would have passport and baggage checks. We kept asking Godson what time the flight was scheduled to leave and he kept saying we had to be there by 10 A.M. Finally, we rounded a curve in the road, and there was our plane sitting in the middle of a small clearing with the engine running. Our bags were quickly loaded into a hatch; we hugged Godson goodbye and ran to the plane, which took off as soon as we were on board with seat belts fastened. The "runway" was an open and bumpy field, and within 15 minutes we landed again, this time at the Serena airstrip, where a few passengers unloaded and a few more boarded. The next stop was Arusha, which has a small military base where local planes land. Our bags were unloaded here and tagged for various destinations. We went through a passport check, then walked around a bit waiting for the next flight. There was some confusion over the luggage, so Phil was summoned to go to the airstrip to identify our luggage, leaving me behind in the terminal. About 15 minutes later another group was escorted to the plane bound for Zanzibar, again leaving me behind. At this point I was getting concerned and started trying to explain to the authorities that I needed to get on the plane to Zanzibar and that Phil was already out there standing by the now loading plane; so finally they allowed me to pass through the gate and board the aircraft. I didn't like being separated from Phil with the possibility of being left behind, as the system was confusing and communication was difficult. We did end up on the correct plane to Zanzibar with all of our luggage on board.

The plane ride was most interesting. The planes that we rode on had European pilots with native African co-pilots. They had open cockpits, and our plane was a prop jet that carried about 20 passengers. The flight was a little under two hours; we flew over the rift valley, and we saw the snow-capped top of Mt. Kilimanjaro for the first time, as it is hidden in the clouds most of the time when viewed from the ground. We also flew over an active volcano that was spewing smoke and ash.

We arrived in Stone Town, Zanzibar, about 2:30 in the afternoon and were met by our new driver from Zenith Tours, who took us first to the ATM and then to the Hotel Tembo, our stop for the night. After that, we were on our own for the rest of the afternoon. The hotel was right on the waterfront and several large commercial ferries were docked nearby. It was also in Old Stone Town, which is an interesting place to walk around in and explore. It was hot and humid, especially after being in the high cool climate of the Serengeti, but it was nice to be able to walk around without being attacked by "fly catchers" or wild animals. We also sat on the beach in a lounge area next to our hotel and sipped cool drinks in the breeze. Later Phil went for a swim in our hotel pool, which was very nice. We ate dinner on the beach that evening, then turned in early after a busy day.

JANUARY 29th

This morning we were met after breakfast by our new local guide and driver who took us on a two-hour walking tour of Stone Town. This turned out to be quite informative and interesting, a totally different experience than we had earlier in Tanzania. We started at the large open market on one side of town, the African equivalent of Pike Place Market in Seattle. There were huge amounts of freshly caught fish. Our guide told us that the fishermen went out at night and by noon all of these fish would be sold out. The beef market section was smaller and consisted of primarily imported meat from Tanzania. There were also large amounts of fruit, vegetables, and spices, as Zanzibar is a "spice island."

Beyond the food market was a section of town consisting of shops with numerous jewelry stores. There were residences located above the shops. In the center of the town were mainly residences, many with beautiful historic old carved doors. We passed a school just getting out of session, and as we worked our way towards the seashore there were churches, mosques, government buildings, and a large museum.

One of the churches was a historical marker for the spot where the slave trade took place. The slaves were taken from Africa by Arabs, then sold to Europeans, primarily the French. Our guide said that there was no evidence that any of these slaves were taken to America. He said the slaves taken to America were from West Africa. Although there are some Anglican and Protestant churches here, as well as a Buddhist Temple, these are far outnumbered by Moslem Mosques, and indeed the Muslim influence here is very strong. In fact, when Phil and I turned on the evening news, it was Al Jazeera in English.

Our Guide explaining the Slave Market

Fig. 11.4 The slave market in Zanzibar.

A History of East Africa, Odhiambo, Ouso & Williams
Longman, England 1977 reprinted twice 1988.
ISBN 0582 60886 4

This was
, an explo
They stay
Zanzibar

"Bound for
America"

After the tour of Stone Town, our driver took us for the one-hour ride to our beach resort hotel. The resort was beautiful, and the Indian Ocean is a pure clear blue color that is difficult to describe. However, even next to the ocean, it was very hot and humid. We arrived too early for check-in, so we went to the open-air restaurant next to the pool for lunch while waiting for our room. The room was lovely, another African-style round BOMA, decorated in luxury. After relaxing and refreshing ourselves, we went to the recreational office to sign Phil up for a scuba excursion the next day. This required a "refresher" course, which he was given in the pool on the spot. After that we had cocktails on the platform deck above the pool which overlooked the ocean. I tried the "Dawa" drink that was recommended by our tour company. It was OK, but not to "rave" about. Later we had dinner at the poolside restaurant where a small band played relaxing African music.

JANUARY 30th

Phil was off by 7:30 this morning for his scuba diving excursion, which went to a nearby offshore island. I spent the day reading and relaxing under a large thatched umbrella by the beach where there was a cool breeze.

Phil returned about 2 P.M.; his report on the diving was that it was good, but not "the best in the world" as it had been described earlier. He saw green sea turtles, moray eel, lionfish, scorpionfish, and many other tropical aquarium fish varieties. The rest of our day was spent much like the day before, just relaxing by the pool and beach. The tour company had advised us that Zanzibar was a good place to relax after going on safari, winding down a bit before the long trek home, and we have to agree that they were correct.

JANUARY 31st

This was our final day in Zanzibar and also Africa, and it wasn't without some small and large issues. Our itinerary took us from Zanzibar to Dar es Salaam and from there to Amsterdam. In order to break up the long flight, we had booked a hotel in Amsterdam for one night, leaving the following day for the final leg of our international flight home. When we went to check out at the resort in Zanzibar, we found they had us booked for an additional night, which instituted a panic call to Zenith Tours to make sure that our driver was picking us up and taking us to the airport today. Everything was reconfirmed, and we actually were able to take the Spice Tour that was part of our itinerary. The guide and driver picked us up at 1 P.M. as scheduled. The spice farm tour turned out to be quite interesting; we saw many of the spices and fruits we had been eating while in Africa. As we were leaving, we received a gift of a handwoven palm leaf basket from the resident farm tour guide, which we unfortunately had to leave behind due to luggage constraints. After the tour we left for the airport.

The plane left on time at 4 P.M. for the 20-minute flight to Dar. Things deteriorated after that, and we will remember the wait at Dar as "the layover from hell." Initially the flight was scheduled to leave at 11:45 P.M., a 7.5-hour layover. We were prepared for this and intended to have dinner, then read and sleep in an air-conditioned waiting area at the airport. HA!!! First, we learned upon arrival at the airport that the plane was delayed by another long 3.5 hours, now scheduled to leave at 3:30 A.M.

The next unpleasant surprise was that we were not allowed to enter the airport until 8 P.M., leaving us in the hot and humid street outside with our luggage for another 3.5 hours. We were able to find a little cafe where we could eat and kill time, but it was also hot, with no AC, only fans.

Finally, at 8 P.M. the door to the main terminal was opened, and we all piled in to wait in line with our luggage for check-in. Another unpleasant surprise; still NO AC! By this time we were baking; it does not cool off at night in this part of Africa and the humidity is unbearable if you are not used to it. Finally, at 10 P.M. we were allowed to check our bags and find a seat in another waiting room in the terminal; still no AC, but I found a place to sit in front of a fan and dry my hair, which was by now wringing wet and sticking to my face. Phil found a place on the floor and almost literally passed out (in sleep). At 3 A.M. the plane arrived; we had one more security check and were escorted into a final waiting room, this one with AC!!! We only stayed there 15 minutes and were thankfully boarded on the plane to Amsterdam after a marathon 11-hour wait in the heat.

The next 10 hours were spent in flight; we had a two-seat row, so room to spread out and rest. We were VERY TIRED after our Dar experience, so we were able to sleep for most of the flight.

FEBRUARY 1st

We landed in Amsterdam at 10 A.M. and managed to make it to the hotel in time for the buffet breakfast which ended at 11 A.M. After eating, cleaning up, and resting, we headed out for some sightseeing in downtown Amsterdam via a bus and subway. We spent the rest of the day visiting the Gassan Diamond Factory and The Rembrandt House. After dinner at our hotel, we had some needed rest before our long flight home in the morning.

Home with our Memories

Epilogue

EXTRA NOTES—SPECIAL MOMENTS

In writing this journal, it became apparent that important impressions and events had been excluded, as they did not fit the exact format of a daily journal. Since these impressions were the basis of the most lasting memories of the trip, I would like to share them in a different format, with a short paragraph or two about each subject.

GODSON

Perhaps the most memorable part of our trip was having Godson as our Guide and becoming acquainted with him over the two weeks that we were together almost constantly. Phil describes him as a "Denzel Washington" type of guy, and that description is a good start. The first quality that struck us when we met him was his openness and sincerity. He was immediately likable, easy to talk to, and easy to get along with. He was meticulous in his personal appearance and in the care of his vehicle. He took great pride in maintaining that vehicle, and at one point the radio antenna was lost when we brushed against a large bush next to the road. Phil and I were certain that the antenna piece was forever lost in the brush, but Godson was persistent about looking until he found it, and it was magically repaired on the following day when he picked us up for our next game drive.

He loved to eat, especially the good food that was prepared for us and shared with the guides. They always packed way too much food for Phil and me in the lunches, and at one point I asked Godson if people really were ever able to eat all of that food. His answer was, "Well, me for example, I always eat all of mine." It was true, and I had to smile. He had no weight problems, so I am sure he used every single calorie he ate. The other funny story about food had to do with a group of Italians who were generally traveling in our footsteps. This was a group of 12 Italian photographers, which included their own Italian Guide. They had hired a driver from the same tour company that employed Godson, so his friends were the drivers for this group. We kept running into this group out on the safari roads. Each time we did, it was after lunch, and Godson passed our leftover packaged and unopened food to these drivers. Finally, he shared the story with us. It seems that the Italians had made no provision for their drivers to eat along the way on the safari. Apparently, it was expected that if you hired a driver and not guides, that you would feed that driver, but the Italians were too cheap to do that. The Italian tour company provided very little food, even for their own customers, the photographers. Sometimes the only lunch was bananas, and when the African drivers complained, they were told that Italian Photographers don't need anything except bananas for lunch. So Godson was feeding them our lunches, which we were happy to share. The other "Italian" story was about camping out. The Italian tour company wanted to save money by having the photographers sleep in campsites some of the nights, so tents and gear had to be provided by the Italian tour company. Well, they provided eight one-person tents for twelve people, which was, of course, a totally untenable situation. So the drivers (3 of them) from Godson's company gave their tents to the Italians, and the drivers slept in their safari vehicles. On at least one occasion, they had to squeeze some of the photographers into an already booked Kikoti Camp, as it would have been too dangerous for them to camp in the open without tents. So we shared some laughs with Godson over the antics of the Italian Photographers and their VERY THRIFTY (some would say Cheap) tour company. After observing the Italians and hearing some stories about the French, we asked Godson how Americans on safari compared with these other European groups. He replied that Americans were wonderful as tourists and that if you couldn't get along with Americans (as guides), then you couldn't get along with anyone. It was reassuring to hear nice things about Americans abroad, and our own experience has been that generally Americans are very polite to their hosts in foreign countries, as well as to their fellow travelers.

A little story about luggage is also amusing. Phil and I were given dire warnings about packing too much for the trip. We were told that the local airlines only allowed one suitcase per person and it had to be of minimal weight and size. We had, therefore, planned and packed very carefully, and even at that, we weren't sure that we hadn't taken too much with us. Then we found that we had the huge safari vehicle to ourselves, so both us and the luggage were swimming in that vehicle. But as the time arrived for us to leave Tanzania and fly to Zanzibar on the local airline, we began to be concerned about whether or not our luggage would be acceptable, so we asked Godson if we were OK with our luggage. He laughed and said, "Oh yes, everyone along the way that had helped with our luggage was really impressed about how lightly we traveled." He then told us about many of the other tourists he had taken on safari, who brought "tons of luggage" with them. At times he had as many as 8 or IO people in his vehicle with all of their luggage. When this happened, the tour company had to give each person a new suitcase of proper size, asking each of them to re-pack, taking only what they absolutely needed in that one bag, and leaving everything else behind in storage with the tour company. We laughed, as it was easy to see how two bags per person for 10 people would never fit in that safari vehicle.

Cameras and pictures were an important feature of our trip, and as mentioned earlier, I had the still camera and Phil was taking movies with a camcorder. We also had a small portable DVD player that ran on batteries, so we were able to view our movies in the evening. When we were camping on the Serengeti, we were able to share some of these movies with Godson. Some of them were truly remarkable, as the telephoto lens brought the action in so much closer than we could see with the naked eye. Godson watched a few of these, then said, "I can't believe I am on this safari with you---it is like a dream!!" The last funny story about photos is what we discovered when we looked at them at home later. One day we came across a male lion in the grassy savannah, and he was very active, although somewhat distant for us to see what was actually taking place. Godson noted that there was also a female present and explained to us that they were probably mating. We took movies of the activity for several minutes until both lions disappeared into the grassy brush. When we viewed this sequence at home, we were amazed to discover that we had actually captured the mating activity. Phil has dubbed this sequence as X-rated for lions (smile).

Our last story about Godson has to do with binoculars. An essential piece of equipment on safari is at least one pair of binoculars. Phil and I were sharing a pair that we brought from home, and Godson had his own. The most important part of a guide job in Africa is being able to spot the animals for your clients on safari. These guides are experts at that, but they very much depend on a good pair of binoculars. Well, during our search for the elusive leopard, Godson mentioned without complaining that he wished his binoculars were a little better, whereupon we loaned him ours to look for the leopards. As the trip progressed, we handed him our binoculars more and more often and found that indeed it made it easier for him to spot the animals. I finally asked him how much a pair like ours would cost in Tanzania, and he responded that binoculars of that quality would not even be available. Ours were not the least expensive, but they also were not the best available, so we were surprised that this essential item would be so far out of reach for a professional safari guide. Phil and I decided that as part of his tip, we needed to give Godson these binoculars when we left, so as we ran for the plane on the grass strip of the Serengeti, we handed the binoculars to him. He later wrote how grateful he was to us, so we are glad that we could give him that gift.

ZANZIBAR

The visit to Zanzibar seemed like a world apart from the stay in Tanzania. Phil and I loved Tanzania; its' people, the geography and scenery, the climate, and the animals. We could not have had a more perfect trip. Then we went to Zanzibar. Here we found the people to be distant and aloof. In Tanzania the people were friendly and open in their communication and inviting to foreigners from all over the world. Zanzibar has beautiful beaches and scenery. It also has an interesting history and culture, but it is much less open and friendly than Tanzania.

COMING TO AMERICA

Godson was clearly interested in coming to America; he had tried once, was turned down for the visa, and was in the process of trying again when we met him. He was so excited and sure that he would make it this time, so when we left, we felt that we might see him again soon. Our own re-entry on return to Seattle took some adjustment. We not only had jet lag but there was an element of returning to reality after spending time in what almost seemed like paradise. For a long time we still felt like we had one foot in Africa---something that is difficult to explain to someone who has never been there but is readily understood by those who have shared that experience. So, in addition to making the adjustment to coming home, I also kept thinking about what our country would seem like to Godson. I tried to imagine what it would be like to walk in his shoes and view America for the first time coming from rural Africa. I tried to imagine what it would seem like driving on freeways at 65 mph after driving in sparse traffic on open roads, most of which were gravel and where driving 35 mph is fast. I tried to imagine what he would think of our tall skyscrapers and crowded downtown streets; I tried to imagine how it would feel to shop in a mall for the first time, with every possible product imaginable being available for sale and reasonably priced. I tried to imagine how it would seem to drive for miles and not see large expanses of open savannas filled with animals living wild and free. And I had to ask myself, would he really like it here? Not that Africa doesn't have its problems; there is high crime in the cities, and disease is a problem, as modern health care is not readily available. However, life is really more simple, and in many ways more beautiful. But we may never know if Godson would like America or not. About two months after we returned, we received the unhappy news that he had been turned down again for the visa. He was very disappointed and said he did not know if he wanted to try a third time. Phil and I shared his disappointment and wished that we could see him again, but we have lost the connection and will have to be satisfied with the memories.

And so ends this story about our journey to Africa. We hope that you have enjoyed sharing it with us through this journal and our photos and that you too might be inspired to visit this amazing land.